Cook from the heart!,

Neil Katz

# LOUKOUMI's CELEBRITY COOKBOOK

## FEATURING FAVORITE CHILDHOOD RECIPES BY OVER 50 CELEBRITIES

Storybook Introduction with CAT CORA

# Nick Katsoris

# Cooking for a Cause

## A minimum of $2 from the sale of each book will be donated to:

**Chefs for Humanity** is an alliance of culinary professionals and educators working in partnership with U.S. and global organizations, providing nutrition education, hunger relief, and emergency and humanitarian aid to reduce hunger across the world. For more information, please visit: **www.chefsforhumanity.org**

*"Loukoumi's Celebrity Cookbook is a fantastic way to get your children excited about helping out and experimenting with you in the kitchen to make delicious and healthful meals from the heart that the whole family can enjoy together."*
**–Celebrity Chef Cat Cora, President & Founder, Chefs for Humanity**

**St. Jude Children's Research Hospital®** is one of the world's premier pediatric cancer research centers. Its mission is to find cures for children with cancer and other catastrophic diseases through research and treatment. At St. Jude, no child is ever turned away for a family's inability to pay. For more information, please visit: **www.stjude.org**

*"The Loukoumi series of books has been wonderful for kids and parents alike. They each have an inspiring message and like the others, Loukoumi's Celebrity Cookbook is a great story with the bonus of being full of delicious recipes. St. Jude Children's Research Hospital is honored to benefit from this project."*
**–Marlo Thomas, National Outreach Director, St. Jude Children's Research Hospital**

# Dedication

To Cat Cora and all the participating celebrities for teaching kids that cooking is fun! May your favorite childhood recipes become the favorites of children all over the world.
And always to Voula, Dean and Julia for making it all worthwhile!

- Nick Katsoris

Copyright © 2011, **Nick Katsoris**
**Dream Day Press/NK Publications/Loukoumi Books**
Loukoumi is a registered trademark.
**All rights reserved.**

**Special thanks to:** Marlo Thomas, Teri Watson and Sarah Newman at St. Jude, Ashley Campbell, Mark Johnson, Karen D'Attore at Chefs for Humanity, Karen and Tom at Strauss Consultants, Shetoli, Atanu, Sarita, Joseph, Dharmesh, and Shipra at Thomson, Sandi, Cathy and Emily at HMI, Jackie and Melinda at Fifteen Minutes, Effie and John at IMC, Jimmy Kapsalis, Jillian Nelson, Alina Tsouristakis, Ron, Dana, Jacki, Denise, Vince, Jonathan and Steve at RJ and Bang, and Bara Voto at Getty Images.

# What Is Your Favorite Childhood Recipe?

Enter the Loukoumi's Secret Ingredient Recipe Contest

The winner will get the chance to cook his or her Favorite Childhood Recipe with Celebrity Chef CAT CORA

For Details Visit:
www.Loukoumi.com

# Storybook Introduction
## Loukoumi's Secret Ingredient

## by Nick Katsoris

One sunny afternoon, Loukoumi and her
friends Fistiki the cat, Dean the dog and
Marika the monkey were playing tag.

"I got you, Dean!"
Loukoumi said.

"You can't catch me!"
Marika called out.
Loukoumi chased Marika
all around the yard.
Finally Loukoumi tagged
her and they both lost
their balance.

They laughed until
they were out
of breath.

Loukoumi then brought her friends inside
her home to cool off.
Fistiki's Aunt Cat Cora was there!
Everyone loved it when Cat came to visit.
She always made something yummy to eat.

Loukoumi's tummy started growling.
"I'm hungry!" Loukoumi said.
"Would you like to cook something with me?" Cat asked.
"Sure, but I don't know how to cook," Loukoumi said.

And Cat responded:
"A pizza pie, a salad, a cake,
cooking is fun, whatever you make.
Perfect to do with family, or a friend,
you'll enjoy yourself from beginning to end.
Brownies, spaghetti or a strawberry tart,
it's always delicious when you cook from the heart!"

"Sounds like fun!" Loukoumi said, "but I don't know WHAT to cook."

Cat had the answer. "Let's make my favorite recipe when I was a kid. It's my Grandma's Italian Cream Cake. She made it for me on my birthday every year!"

So they decided to bake Cat's cake!

First, Marika opened up the cookbook to the correct page so they could get everything ready.

Fistiki took out the baking pan.

Dean grabbed the measuring cup.

And Loukoumi carried the spoons to the counter.

11

"Always measure the ingredients carefully," said Cat, as she helped Fistiki measure just enough sugar.
Fistiki poured it into a large mixing bowl all by himself.

Now it was Loukoumi's turn to measure the flour. The bag of flour was brand new, and it wouldn't open!
Loukoumi pulled and pulled and poof! The bag exploded and a cloud of flour floated all over the kitchen.

Cat Cora and Loukoumi were coughing.

Cat then said, "You can't make anything delicious without making a little bit of a mess."

Loukoumi then got the eggs out of the refrigerator, but she didn't see the puddle of water on the floor.

Loukoumi slipped and the eggs flew out of the carton. A few crashed down on the floor, but Marika caught two in mid-air.

"Nice catch!" Cat said.

Now it was time to add the milk. Loukoumi picked up the jug and tried to pour it into the measuring cup.

It was very heavy. Loukoumi didn't think she would be able to do it. Some milk splattered on the counter, but Fistiki helped and together they poured the milk into the measuring cup.

"Nice teamwork," Cat said. "The secret ingredient is never give up!"

It was time to mix all the ingredients. Everyone took turns.

"This is cool," Dean said, swooshing the ingredients together.

"And so tasty!" Fistiki said, licking his lips.

Cat poured the batter into a cake pan and said, "Now we place the pan in the oven for thirty minutes. Remember, it is very hot, so always ask an adult to help you."

Soon the cake was done and Cat took it out of the oven.

After the cake cooled, everyone had a
piece. It was delicious!

Between bites, Loukoumi said:
"A pizza pie, a salad, a cake,
cooking is fun, whatever you make.
Perfect to do with family, or a friend,
I enjoyed myself from beginning to end.
Brownies, spaghetti or a strawberry tart,
it's always delicious when you cook from the heart!
So keep at your recipe,
raise your measuring cup
because the secret ingredient is
never give up!"

The End

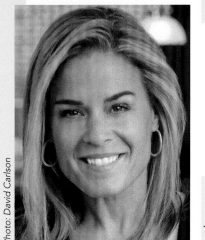

Photo: David Carlson

# Alma's Italian Cream Cake

## Cat Cora

*Celebrity Chef;*
*President & Founder of Chefs for Humanity*

*"My mother's mother, Alma, was a beacon - the one person in the family to whom all of us were drawn in good times and in bad. She served this cake for anniversaries, funerals, weddings, baptisms, and especially birthdays. When I was growing up, birthdays in my family were major events; my parents were of the 'This is your big day' mentality. My mom would cook exactly what we wanted for dinner, and Alma, already knowing the answer, would ask us what kind of cake we wanted. We never hesitated. 'Grandmom, your Italian Cream Cake!' Off she'd go to make a moist, silky cake, with a frosting so luscious and creamy that you couldn't keep your fingers away from it no matter how hard you tried. Two things in my memory never fail to make me happy when I think of them: My Alma, and this cake."*

*— Cat Cora*

## Ingredients

### Alma's Italian Cream Cake
Serves 10 to 16

- 2 cups cake flour
- 1 teaspoon baking soda
- ½ teaspoon salt
- 12 tablespoons (1 ½ sticks) unsalted butter, softened to room temperature
- 2 cups granulated sugar
- 5 large eggs, yolks and whites separated, at room temperature
- 1 cup buttermilk
- 1 teaspoon vanilla extract
- 1 cup sweetened shredded coconut (angel flake)
- 1 cup finely chopped walnuts, toasted

### Cream Cheese Frosting

- 1 cup chopped walnuts, toasted
- 1 8-ounce package cream cheese, softened
- 8 tablespoons (1 stick) unsalted butter, softened
- 1 tablespoon vanilla extract
- 4 cups (1 pound) confectioners' sugar, sifted

## Instructions

### For the cakes:

1. Place a rack in the middle of the oven and preheat oven to 350 degrees.

2. Prepare 2 round 9-inch cake pans by greasing and flouring them or by cutting a circle of parchment to fit each pan, greasing the pan, fitting the parchment into place, and then greasing the parchment.

3. Sift the flour, baking soda, and salt into a medium bowl and set aside. In the bowl of a stand or with a hand mixer, cream the butter and 1 ½ cups of the sugar until light and fluffy. Add egg yolks one at a time beating well after each addition. Add the sifted dry ingredients and buttermilk in thirds to the creamed mixture, beating on medium speed after each addition and wiping the sides of the bowl down with a rubber spatula. Add vanilla, coconut and nuts and mix well.

4. In a separate bowl, whip the egg whites with cleaned beaters, slowly adding the remaining ½ cup of sugar and beating until the whites form stiff peaks but are not dry. Carefully, fold one third of the egg white mixture into the batter until all is incorporated. Fold in the next third of the egg whites and, when that's incorporated, gently fold in the last third.

5. Divide the batter evenly into the 2 prepared pans.

6. Bake until the top is golden brown and a wooden toothpick comes out clean when inserted in the middle of the cake, about 30 to 35 minutes. Let the cakes cool completely before removing them from the pans.

### For the cream cheese frosting:

1. Beat the cream cheese, butter, and vanilla at medium speed with an electric mixer until creamy. Add powdered sugar, one cup at a time, beating at low speed until blended. When all the ingredients are incorporated, beat the frosting at high speed until smooth. Stir in ½ cup of the toasted walnuts.

2. Ice the sides and top of one cake first before placing the other cake on top. Then ice the second cake. Place the frosted cake in the refrigerator to firm up the frosting. Remove the cake from the refrigerator about 30 minutes before serving, and press the remaining ½ cup of walnuts into the frosting on top.

**To toast the walnuts:**
Toast the chopped walnuts in a shallow baking pan at 325 degrees for about 5 to 7 minutes or until the nuts are fragrant. Remove the pan from the oven and let the nuts cool.

# Now Try These Favorite Childhood Recipes:

## WEEKEND BREAKFASTS

## LUNCHTIME FAVORITES

## AFTER SCHOOL SNACKS

## FAMILY MEALS

## DELICIOUS DESSERTS

# Weekend Breakfasts

# Cinnamon Toast

## John Aniston

*Actor, Days of our Lives*

*"It's sugar and spice, nuf said!"— John Aniston*

### Ingredients
- 2 slices of white bread, lightly toasted
- 2 pats of butter
- Sugar
- Cinnamon

### Instructions
1. Toast the bread lightly.

2. Then spread butter across each slice covering the piece in its entirety.

3. Sprinkle a dash of sugar with a dash of cinnamon on top of that and enjoy!

Photo: Fred Goudon

# Pain Perdu (French Toast)

## Gilles Marini
*Actor*

*"'Pain Perdu' means lost bread because the French buy fresh baguettes everyday, and instead of throwing away the leftover bread, we use it to make 'Pain Perdu.' The bread is moist inside and slightly crunchy on the outside. I can still taste it in my mouth (some whipped cream is a plus)."*
*— Gilles Marini*

### Ingredients
- 1 baguette, one day old
- 2 cups of milk
- 3 eggs
- Vanilla sugar or regular sugar with vanilla extract
- Butter
- Powdered sugar

### Instructions
1. Have two bowls ready. In the first bowl put the milk and sweeten it with the sugar and the vanilla (if you did not find vanilla sugar). Make sure it is sweet enough by tasting. In the other bowl, put the beaten eggs.

2. Then carefully with help, slice the baguette as large as one quarter of the baguette (needs to be a circle slice, cut on the vertical part of the baguette), put some butter in the pan, take a slice of bread and let the fun begin.

3. Dip it in the milk on one side, dip it in the milk on the other side (the inside of the bread needs to be wet by the mix). Then dip it on both sides in the bowl with the eggs and then put it in the buttered pan. When it becomes a little brown, turn it and do the same.

4. Now that your French Toast is on a plate, sprinkle some powdered sugar on top and enjoy the French Toast from France.

# Egg and Toast Best Breakfast!

## Bridgit Mendler

### *Actress, Good Luck Charlie*

*"My eggs on toast recipe is great because it's one of those simple pleasures that doesn't take a lot of work to make, but it always tastes like such a special treat. I love lathering on the ketchup just like I did when I was eight!"*

*— Bridgit Mendler*

## Ingredients
- 1 egg
- 1 piece of bread (whatever type, your choice!)
- 3 slices of cheese
- 1 tablespoon ketchup

## Instructions

1. In a small frying pan cook egg sunnyside up. I personally like my egg a little more well done so I cook it on both sides, but that's up to you!

2. While egg is cooking, insert bread into toaster. Again, the level of toasting is up to you. I like my toast a little on the lighter side.

3. Once the bread is toasted, lay three slices of cheese on toast.

4. Once egg is cooked, lay egg on top of cheese.

5. Spread ketchup over egg.

6. (Optional) Cut egg on toast in half for easier eating.

27

# Betty's Biscuits

## Nancy O'Dell
*Co-Anchor, Entertainment Tonight*

*"I LOVE these biscuits because they remind me so much of my sweet Mom. That's why my family has named them Betty's Biscuits after my Mom. She would make them so often and always on special holidays like Thanksgiving and Christmas. So even though my Mom is no longer with us, when I add her biscuits to a meal, it makes me feel like she is there in a way because memories flood back of all those great times we had together."*

*— Nancy O'Dell*

## Ingredients
- 2 cups self-rising flour
- 2 teaspoons baking powder
- 2 tablespoons confectioners' sugar (10x) or granulated sugar
- ⅓ to ½ cup solid Crisco
- 1 cup buttermilk

## Instructions
1. Mix flour, sugar, baking powder and Crisco (crunch up with hands).
2. Add buttermilk and stir.
3. Roll out on waxed paper with rolling pin.
4. Cut with cutter.
5. Bake on greased sheets in pre-heated oven - 400-425 degrees until brown.

*Cover Photo: Kal Yee*

# French Toast Cups with Fresh Fruit

## Rachael Ray

*Author and Television Personality*

*"This sweet breakfast treat tastes delicious all year round, but it's easy enough for kids to make (with just a little help from a grown-up helper!) for a special breakfast-in-bed treat for Mom or Dad."*

— *Rachael Ray*

## Ingredients

**Serves 4-6**

- Nonstick cooking spray
- 3 eggs
- 1 tablespoon (a splash) milk (eyeball it)
- 2 teaspoons (about half a palmful) cinnamon
- Dash of vanilla extract, optional
- Dash of fresh nutmeg, optional
- 6 slices whole grain sandwich bread
- 1 pint fresh berries such as strawberries, blueberries, blackberries or raspberries
- 1 cup Greek yogurt, regular or low-fat
- Maple syrup or honey, to drizzle over

## Instructions

1. Preheat oven to 375 degrees.
2. Spray the inside of each cup of a 6-cup muffin tin with nonstick cooking spray and set aside.
3. In a medium-size mixing bowl, whisk together the eggs, milk, cinnamon, vanilla and nutmeg. Cut a slit in the corner of each slice of bread from the middle of the slice to the edge.
4. Dip each slice of bread in the egg mixture, then lightly press it into a cup of the muffin tin, overlapping the pieces where you cut the slit to make it fit into the cup without tearing. Bake the French Toast Cups for 12-14 minutes, until they are light golden brown.
5. Allow the cups to cool slightly in the muffin tin before removing them. To serve, arrange the cups on a platter, fill each one with fresh fruit and a dollop of yogurt.
6. Drizzle with maple syrup or honey.

Photo: Miranda Penn-Turin

# Monkey Bread

## Hillary Scott

*Grammy Award Winning Entertainer,
Lady Antebellum*

> *"This is one of my favorite recipes because I can remember my Mom and Grandma Rose making Monkey Bread for me as a little girl. It's like the good gooey part of cinnamon rolls and fun to pull apart! Perfect for sharing with friends and family."*
>
> *— Hillary Scott*

### Ingredients
- 4 cans of biscuits
- 2 cups sugar
- 3 tablespoons cinnamon
- 1 ½ sticks butter or margarine

### Instructions

1. Preheat the oven to 350 degrees.

2. Cut each biscuit into quarters.

3. Combine 1 cup sugar and 2 tablespoons of cinnamon along with biscuits in a zip lock bag. Shake to coat each biscuit.

4. Put biscuit quarters into a tube pan.

5. Bring butter, 1 cup sugar and 1 tablespoon cinnamon to a boil.

6. Pour heated mix over biscuits. Bake for 35-40 minutes.

7. Pull pieces apart to serve.

# Oprah's Corn Fritters

## Oprah Winfrey

*Television Pioneer; CEO, OWN*

*"These southern-style fritters are just right with maple syrup, fruit syrup or honey."*

*— Oprah Winfrey*

## Ingredients
**Serves 4**

- ⅔ cup yellow cornmeal
- ⅓ cup self-rising flour
- 1 cup buttermilk
- 1 egg, beaten
- 2 ears corn, shucked, or ½ cup frozen or canned corn
- 2 tablespoons melted unsalted butter, optional
- Milk or water, if needed
- Pam

## Instructions

1. Microwave the corn on high for 2 or 3 minutes. Slice off the kernels, and set them aside.

2. In a bowl, mix the cornmeal and the flour well, using a wire whisk. This will make your fritters very light. In a separate bowl, whisk together the buttermilk and the egg.

3. Gradually add the wet ingredients to the dry. Don't worry if the batter isn't completely combined; you want to be careful not to overmix it. Fold in the corn and add the butter if desired. If the result is thicker than pancake batter, thin it with a little milk or water.

4. Heat a skillet or a griddle to medium, spray with Pam, and add spoonfuls of batter. Cook the fritters for 2 minutes per side. A great way to tell if they're ready to turn is to look for little bubbles all over the surface. You might have to make a few fritters before they start coming out perfectly.

5. Serve with honey or your favorite syrup.

# Lunchtime Favorites

# Favorite Quinoa Salad

## Jennifer Aniston
### *Emmy Award Winning Actress*

*"This is a really simple salad, but so delicious, and all these beautiful, healthy ingredients make it one of my favorites."*

— *Jennifer Aniston*

## Ingredients
- ½ cup quinoa
- 1 cup water
- Pinch of salt
- 1 bunch flat leaf parsley, washed and chopped (thick stems removed)
- 4 Persian cucumbers peeled in strips, seeded and diced
- 2 medium tomatoes, diced
- 1 ripe but slightly firm avocado, diced
- 2-3 tablespoons extra virgin olive oil
- Salt and pepper to taste

## Instructions
1. In a small saucepan bring water and salt to a boil.

2. Stir in quinoa, cover and lower the heat to simmer. Cook for 15 minutes.

3. Put quinoa into a medium size mixing bowl and cool.

4. Add parsley, cucumbers, tomatoes, avocado and oil to quinoa.

5. Mix and season to taste with salt and pepper.

# English Muffin Pizzas

## Alexis Christoforous
### CBS News Anchor & National Correspondent

*"Every Wednesday I would make these adorable mini-pizzas with my Mom after school. They're still a comforting and tasty treat that I now enjoy making with my own children."*

*— Alexis Christoforous*

### Ingredients
- 1 whole-wheat English Muffin, split
- 1 jar of pizza sauce (homemade or store bought)
- ¼ cup shredded part-skim mozzarella cheese (try sharp cheddar, Monterey Jack or feta to mix it up!)
- Chopped fresh basil, for decorating
- Toppings (optional) - make a funny pizza face with pepperoni circles for eyes, peppers for a mouth and pitted olives or a broccoli crown for the nose

### Instructions
1. Preheat the oven to 450 degrees. Line a small baking sheet with foil.

2. Place the English Muffin halves cut-side up on the baking sheet. Top each with sauce (be careful not to put too much, or you'll have soggy pizzas).

3. Sprinkle with the mozzarella cheese and any toppings you like.

4. Bake for 10 to 12 minutes, or until the cheese is melted and beginning to brown.

5. Sprinkle with basil and make your own family memories!

# Vegan Sliders

## Ellen DeGeneres
### Talk Show Host, Ellen

*"I love this recipe because it's a compassionate way to eat and the sliders taste even better than ones made with beef. And they're half the size of a regular burger so you can eat like 12 of them."*

*— Ellen DeGeneres*

## Ingredients
- 1 firm avocado
- ½ head of iceberg lettuce
- 1 small jar dill pickle slices
- 3 thinly sliced roma tomatoes
- ¼ red onion, very thinly sliced
- 6 slices tempeh bacon (optional)
- 12 vegan veggie patties
- ½ teaspoon EVOO (extra virgin olive oil)
- 1 bottle of vegan Thousand Island dressing (Follow Your Heart brand)
- 12 wheat buns or wheat dinner rolls, 3" each

## Instructions
1. Pre-heat oven to 350 degrees. Defrost veggie patties according to package. Meanwhile prep everything you need to assemble the sliders.
2. Cut avocado in quarters and discard the skins and pit. Cut each avocado quarter into 6 thin slices, then gently fan them out onto a plate and reserve. Cut 12 uniform pieces of iceberg lettuce about 3" in diameter. Place them on a plate and reserve.
3. Remove about 24 pickle slices from the jar and using a paper towel, gently squeeze them dry. Using a sharp serrated knife slice the tomatoes into thin circles. Each tomato should easily yield 8 slices minimum. Lay out each slice onto a paper towel to remove excess moisture. Slice the red onion as thinly as possible and reserve.
4. Cut each piece of bacon in half and bake them on an ungreased cookie sheet at 350 degrees until they are hot and crisp.
5. Using a cookie cutter or a small glass cup cut out 2.5" to 3" patties from the defrosted veggie patties. Reserve the trimmings for another use. Cook all the patties in a hot pan with the EVOO. Reserve the patties warm. At the same time, toast each bun in a dry hot pan or with a small amount of vegan butter.

## Assembly
Lay out 6 buns open face, and spread a small amount of Thousand Island on each side. Place patties on the bottom. Then 2 slices of tempeh bacon, 2 slices of pickles, 2 slices of tomato, a few slices of onion, 2 pieces of avocado, and one piece of iceberg lettuce followed by the top bun. Repeat the process with the remaining 6 buns and place the sliders on a platter and serve.

35

# Grilled Cheese Sandwich

## Carrie Ann Inaba

### Judge, Dancing with the Stars

*"Grilled Cheese sandwiches are still my favorite food and I loved them when I was growing up in Hawaii. You can eat a grilled cheese sandwich for breakfast, lunch and dinner. And they taste great no matter what time of day it is."*

*— Carrie Ann Inaba*

## Things you will need
- Small microwavable bowl to melt the butter in
- Spatula
- Frying pan
- Plate

## Ingredients
- Sliced cheese - American slices always made me happy because I loved taking off the plastic wrapper. If you want to get fancy and experiment, you can use sliced cheddar cheese, pepper jack or even Swiss!
- 2 slices of your favorite bread. My personal favorite was sourdough bread, mainly because the pieces were bigger which meant my sandwich would be bigger and last longer. But you can use whole wheat, or white bread, or any type of bread that you have available to you.
- 1 tablespoon butter.

## Instructions
1. Melt the tablespoon of butter in the microwave. When it's soft and liquid like, spread the butter on one side of each piece of bread (These will face away from the cheese).

2. Put your cheese slices of choice in between the pieces of bread. Now you should have a cheese sandwich with buttery bread facing the outside. Put the frying pan halfway between medium and high. Put the sandwich on the frying pan and let it get slightly browned. Flip over and do the same to the other side.

3. When both sides are at the right color golden brown, remove and cut on a diagonal. Put on a plate and enjoy!!!!

**Grilled cheese sandwiches go great with the following foods:**
- Soup
- Chili
- French Fries
- Potato Chips
- Pickles
- Onion Rings

# Mini Mexican Pizzas

## Honorable Sandra Day O'Connor
### United States Supreme Court Justice

*"Here is a simple recipe that we used on occasion at the Lazy B Ranch."*
*— Honorable Sandra Day O'Connor*

### Ingredients
- 6 small (6 inches each) corn tortillas
- 1 can (16 ounces) fat-free refried beans
- 6 tablespoons already-shredded Mexican-style cheese
- 6 tablespoons frozen corn kernels
- 1 can (4 ounces) mild chopped green chilies, optional
- Salsa, optional
- Sour cream, reduced fat, optional

### Instructions
1. Preheat oven to 450 degrees.

2. Place the tortillas on an 11-by-17 inch baking sheet (the edges may overlap slightly). Divide the beans evenly among the tortillas. Using a rubber spatula, spread them to within half an inch of the edges. Sprinkle 1 tablespoon cheese and 1 tablespoon corn over each tortilla. Drain the chilies and divide them evenly over the tortillas.

3. Bake the tortillas 5 to 6 minutes or until the cheese is melted and the tortillas are steaming.

4. Remove the baking sheet from the oven, and using a wide metal or plastic spatula, transfer each tortilla to a serving plate. Serve at once, topping with salsa and sour cream at the table, if desired.

5. Cook's note: One pizza is usually sufficient, but larger appetites will require two. This recipe is easily doubled or tripled. Makes 4 to 6 servings.

37

# Suite Life Monkey Sandwiches

## Brenda Song

*Actress, The Suite Life on Deck; The Social Network*

*"These are sandwiches I've been making for the Sprouse twins since they were 11. I call them Monkey Sandwiches because it gives us all energy, so it turned us all into crazy monkeys - haha."*

— *Brenda Song*

### Ingredients

- 2 pieces of whole wheat toast
- ½ banana
- Peanut butter
- Honey

### Instructions

1. It's so simple. Toast 2 pieces of whole wheat bread.

2. While the bread is in the toaster, slice up half a banana.

3. Spread peanut butter on each slice of bread and then place the slices of banana on top.

4. Drizzle honey over the slices of banana.

5. Place one side of toast on the other and VOILA! Quick, easy and healthy!

# Alma Wahlberg's Potato Salad

## Mark Wahlberg
*Award Winning Actor and Producer*

> *"My parents worked multiple jobs to put food on the table for me and my eight siblings. This potato salad was always a favorite of ours."*
> — *Mark Wahlberg*

## Ingredients

- 4 pounds potatoes
- 6 eggs
- 6 celery sticks
- 1 purple onion
- 1 green pepper
- 1 small jar of kosher dill stacker pickles
- Mayonnaise
- Celery salt
- Parsley flakes
- Garlic powder
- Salt and pepper

## Instructions

1. Boil potatoes and hard boil eggs.

2. Potatoes are done when you can slide a fork into them easily. Set aside and let cool. Then peel and cut up into a large bowl.

3. Chop small: onions, peppers, celery, and 8 stacker pickles.

4. Add spices to taste. Add mayonnaise.

5. Mix all ingredients together.

39

# After School Snacks

# Easy Guacamole with Corn Chip Scoops

## Beyoncé

*Grammy Award Winning Entertainer*

*"I love avocado. It's one of my healthy snack favorites."*

— *Beyoncé*

## Ingredients

- 2 ripe avocados (make sure they are a bit soft to the touch)
- 1 small onion (ask your parents to chop it finely for you)
- 1 clove garlic (you can use a small amount of crushed garlic)
- 1 small tomato (get some help to chop this)
- 1 ½ tablespoons lime juice
- Salt and pepper to taste
- Corn chip scoops

## Instructions

1. Peel avocados and remove the pit.

2. Smash with a spoon in a large bowl.

3. Add onion, garlic, tomato, lime juice and a pinch of salt and pepper. Mix it well.

4. Cover with plastic wrap and place in the refrigerator for about 20 minutes.

5. Fill corn chip scoops with guacamole and enjoy!

# Fried Cauliflowers & Sfihas (Meat Tarts)

## Celine Dion

### Grammy Award Winning Entertainer

*"I'm delighted and proud to be able to share these favorite recipes of mine, which were a gift to me from René's late mother, Mrs. Alice Angélil. I hope that you enjoy them as much as our family does!"*

— *Celine Dion*

## Ingredients

### FRIED CAULIFLOWERS

- 2 large cauliflowers
- Oil for frying
- Salt (to taste)
- Special Arabian Pepper (finely milled white and black pepper, cardamom, nutmeg, 4-spices, clover and cinnamon. Blend portions of each spice to your personal taste)

## Instructions

1. Blanch the cauliflower in a pot for about 10 minutes in salted water.

2. Remove from pot, break the cauliflower into flowerets and pat dry on a paper towel.

3. Heat oil in frying pan to 375 degrees. Fry cauliflower for a few minutes and then remove and pat dry again.

4. Season with Arabian Pepper (to taste).

### SFIHAS (Meat Tarts)

- 1 container of Pillsbury refrigerated Crescent Dinner Rolls

### For Stuffing

- 1 pound of ground veal
- 1 medium sized onion, finely chopped
- ¼ cup plain yogurt
- 2 tablespoons of roasted pine nuts
- 1 egg
- Salt (to taste)
- Arabian Pepper (see Fried Cauliflowers)

## Instructions

1. Remove Pillsbury dough from container and divide each triangle strip in half. From each half triangle, shape dough into 3" diameter circular tarts and flatten the edges. Leave the center thicker.

2. Mix all of the stuffing ingredients with your hands and spread this mixture on the tarts (Sfihas) to within ¼ inch of the edges.

3. Place Sfihas on a greased cookie sheet and bake for 7-10 minutes on the lower grill. Then move to the upper grill and bake for an additional 5 minutes.

For Celine Dion's Stuffed Vine Leaves Recipe visit:
**www.Loukoumi.com**

# Greek Yogurt

## Olympia Dukakis
*Academy Award Winning Actress*

> *"My recipe is a favorite childhood memory."*
>
> — *Olympia Dukakis*

### Ingredients
- One sweet, sweet white-haired Yia-Yia (Grandmother)
- 1 teaspoon raw sugar
- 1 small slice Greek bread
- 1 cup Greek yogurt

### Instructions
1. Take one small slice of Greek bread and pull it apart into small pieces.

2. Next, take 1 cup Greek yogurt drained through cheesecloth over the sink for 4 hours.

3. Add 1 teaspoon raw sugar and mix all together.

4. Place in front of child, napkin on lap.

5. Accompanied by a story of life in Asia Minor. Preceded by a short prayer.

Photo: Troy Word

# Ritz Cracker Sandwiches

## Gloria Gaynor
### Grammy Award Winning Entertainer

*"One of my fondest memories of my Mom is this snack she used to make for us on Saturday evenings when we would watch a show called 'The Not For Nervous People Theater.' The snack was two sets of sandwiches on Ritz crackers."*

*— Gloria Gaynor*

### Ingredients
**Peanut Butter & Jelly Ritz Sandwiches**

- Peanut butter
- Jelly
- Ritz crackers

### Instructions

Spread the peanut butter and jelly on the Ritz crackers. You can eat them with a single cracker or for a sandwich put another cracker on top!

### Tuna Salad Ritz Sandwiches

- 1 can tuna fish, drained
- 2 boiled eggs, diced
- 2 tablespoons of sweet pickle relish
- 3 to 4 tablespoons of Hellmann's mayonnaise
- Ritz crackers

### Instructions

Mix the ingredients all together. Spread it on top of the crackers and enjoy!

# Jay Leno's Uncle Louie's Chicken Wings Marinara

## Jay Leno

*Host, The Tonight Show with Jay Leno*

*"My uncle always told me 'Someday you'll have to make a dinner for 20 guys, and this is what you'll make.'"*

*— Jay Leno*

### Ingredients
- 2-3 dozen chicken wings
- 1 can Italian plum tomatoes
- Olive oil
- Garlic or garlic powder
- Durkee's Hot Sauce
- Salt
- Parsley

### Instructions

1. Cook chicken wings by broiling them, or lightly flouring and deep frying them in safflower or peanut oil.

2. Heat ⅛ inch of olive oil in a pan, add garlic powder or crushed garlic to taste. Mash one can of whole plum tomatoes through a sieve and cook in the olive oil. Add a few teaspoons of chopped parsley and salt to taste – then cook about 20 minutes.

3. At the end of this cooking time, add Durkee's Hot Sauce (put a little or a lot, depending on how hot or mild your taste), but put in at least 2 tablespoons or the sauce won't be as tasty. Add a little garlic powder and cook another 3-4 minutes.

4. In a bowl, toss the chicken wings with ½ cup of the sauce and serve with the remaining sauce on the side to dip the wings into.

# Chocolate Covered Loukoumi Candy

## Loukoumi
### *Children's Book Star*

*"A sweet and delicious treat! Definitely one of my childhood favorites and this candy is named after me too!"*

— *Loukoumi*

### Ingredients
- 1 box of Loukoumi candy (in your favorite flavor - mine are the vanilla!)
- Chocolate
- Oil or butter

### Instructions
1. Take some loukoumi pieces from the box and cut to desired size.

2. Remove the icing sugar with a brush or steam (if using steam make sure to dry them thoroughly).

3. Melt the chocolate (milk, dark or white) in a Bain Marie, or a double boiling pan.

4. Add a few drops of oil or butter if you want an extra sheen on the chocolate.

5. Put loukoumi candy in the chocolate and cover the pieces all over.

6. Cut some baking paper to the size of a baking tray and place a grid on top.

7. Carefully remove the delights from the chocolate using a skewer.

8. Place on top of grid for chocolate to set. Place in the fridge to speed up the process.

# Asparagus Rollups

## Bailee Madison
### *Actress, Wizards of Waverly Place*

*"When people take their first bite, their eyes get huge and they all say, 'Mmm, what are these?' I love knowing they enjoy them."*
— *Bailee Madison*

## Ingredients

- 24 fresh asparagus spears
- 1 (8-ounce) package cream cheese, softened
- 1 (4-ounce) package crumbled blue cheese
- 2 tablespoons mayonnaise
- 1 tablespoon fresh chives, chopped
- 12 bread slices, trimmed
- 12 thinly sliced deli ham slices
- ¼ cup butter or margarine, melted
- Paprika

## Instructions

1. Snap off tough ends of asparagus. Arrange asparagus in a steamer basket over boiling water. Cover and steam 4 to 6 minutes or until crisp-tender. Remove from steamer and cool on paper towels.

2. Stir together cream cheese, blue cheese, mayonnaise and chives.

3. Roll each bread slice with a rolling pin to flatten.

4. Spread 1 side of each slice with 2 tablespoons cream cheese mixture and top each with 1 ham slice. Place 2 asparagus spears, tips pointed toward opposite ends, on 1 end of each bread slice; roll up, and place, seam side down, on a greased baking sheet. Brush with butter; sprinkle with paprika.

5. Bake at 400 degrees for 12 minutes or until golden. Serve immediately.

# Fancy Pizza

## Amy Poehler
*Actress, Parks & Recreation*

*"Sometimes it's fun to get fancy."*

*— Amy Poehler*

### Ingredients
- Construction paper
- Glue
- Sparkles
- Paper plates
- Your Mom's pretty dress or your Dad's tie
- Imagination
- Pizza

### Instructions

1. Go to your Mom and Dad, or someone you love who is bigger than you, and ask if you can borrow their fancy clothes.

2. Put on fancy clothes and laugh.

3. Take pictures.

4. Mix together the construction paper and glue and sparkles and make fancy placemats. Let placemats sit to dry.

5. Walk over to phone and order pizza.

6. When the pizza arrives make sure an adult gives the delivery person a 20 percent tip.

7. Put pizza on plate. Put plate on placemat. Eat in a very fancy way. Take more pictures. Laugh. Enjoy!

# Chocolate Crackers

## Taylor Swift
### Grammy Award Winning Entertainer

*"These have always been one of my favorites, and they're so easy to make!"*

*— Taylor Swift*

### Ingredients
- 1 cup brown sugar
- 1 cup butter
- 1 box Club crackers
- 1 small bag Nestle's chocolate chips

### Instructions
1. Line cookie sheet with foil. Lay Club crackers on foil to cover the sheet completely.

2. Bring butter and sugar to a boil over medium-high heat in saucepan. Stir frequently and allow to boil for at least 5 minutes or until slightly thickened.

3. Pour thickened mixture evenly over crackers. Sprinkle chocolate chips evenly over hot butter/sugar. Wait 5 minutes for chips to melt. Spread chocolate with knife or spatula to cover surface evenly.

4. Refrigerate for 1 hour.

5. Lift foil to remove entire sheet of crackers. Break apart into cookie-sized pieces. Store in refrigerator.

# Betty's Chicken Wings

## Betty White

*Emmy Award winning Television Legend*

> *"This recipe is so simple, but it's also so good. I have it a couple of times every week."*
>
> — *Betty White*

## Ingredients
- 3 pounds chicken wings
- 1 stick margarine
- 1 cup soy sauce
- 1 cup brown sugar
- ¾ cup water
- ½ teaspoon dry mustard

## Instructions
1. Arrange wings in shallow baking pan.
2. Heat margarine, soy sauce, sugar, water and mustard until margarine and sugar melt. Cool.
3. Pour over wings and marinate at least 2 hours, turning once or twice.
4. Bake in same pan at 375 degrees for 1 ¼ to 1 ½ hours, turning occasionally.
5. Drain on paper towels.

# Family Meals

# Spaghetti Tacos

## Miranda Cosgrove
*Actress, iCarly*

*"Okay, some might say my brother Spencer on iCarly is a little DIFFERENT. But, sometimes he does things that are weird AND good -- like make Spaghetti Tacos. Who else would put together crunchy taco shells with spaghetti and make it soooo delish!?!? So, I thought I'd share his awesome Spaghetti Tacos recipe with all of you!"*
*— Miranda Cosgrove*

### Ingredients
- Taco shells
- Spaghetti
- Meat sauce
- 1 BIG spoon

### Instructions
1. Get taco shells.
2. Get spaghetti (with meat sauce).
3. Get a BIG spoon.
4. Use the BIG spoon to put spaghetti into taco shells.
5. Eat.

# Pastitsio (Greek Lasagna)

## Nick Gregory
### FOX-5 Meteorologist

*"Holidays were always special growing up in a close Greek family. Aside from traditional foods such as turkey, ham, stuffing, mashed and sweet potatoes, we would get to enjoy special Greek dishes too. One of my favorites is Pastitsio. A nice treat would be when I would come home from school on an average day and I would immediately sniff the aroma of Pastitsio cooking in the oven. I'd have to stop and think, 'Was this a holiday?' Then I would realize it was just a special treat from Mom."*

*— Nick Gregory*

## Ingredients

**Meat sauce**
- 2 pounds chopped meat
- 2 tablespoons olive oil
- 2 medium chopped onions
- 1 can tomato paste
- 1 cup of white wine
- Salt to taste

**Bechamel sauce**
- ¾ cup butter
- ¼ teaspoon nutmeg (optional)
- ¾ cup flour
- Salt and pepper to taste
- 6 cups scalded milk
- 6 eggs

**Pasta**
- 2 boxes of ziti pasta
- 1 stick of butter
- Grated Parmesan cheese
- 3 tablespoons of milk
- 2 eggs

## Instructions

1. **Meat Sauce:** Heat oil and sauté onions. Add chopped meat, sauté and then add tomato paste, wine and salt. Simmer over medium heat for 15 minutes. Set aside. Pour excess oil out.

2. **Bechamel Sauce:** Melt butter. Add flour. Cook mixture of butter and flour for approximately 10 minutes until smooth on low heat while stirring constantly. Add the 6 cups of scalded milk slowly and stir with a whisk until smooth and thick. Stir in the 6 beaten eggs slowly.

3. **Pasta:** Cook pasta in boiling salted water. Drain. Melt butter and add pasta. In a separate bowl beat the 2 eggs and the 3 tablespoons of milk together.

4. Stir and layer half the pasta in a 10"×15"×3" baking pan. Sprinkle with grated Parmesan cheese and pour the mixture of 2 eggs beaten with 3 tablespoons of milk (so pasta doesn't stick in the pan).

5. Layer meat sauce on top of the first layer of pasta. Sprinkle more grated Parmesan cheese on top of meat sauce. Top with the remaining pasta. Add a little more grated cheese on top of pasta. Add Bechamel sauce over entire pan.

6. Cook in 350 degree preheated oven for 1 hour or until golden brown and puffed.

# Fresh Pasta with Bolognese Ragu

## Neil Patrick Harris

*Actor, How I Met Your Mother*

*"Since I'm not a cook myself, and my better half David is a chef with his own catering company (Gourmet, M.D.), I asked him to give up his recipe for my very favorite meal - pasta bolognese. It's the best - hearty and full of flavor. And the fresh pasta really makes a difference. I could eat it for every meal."*

*— Neil Patrick Harris*

## Ingredients

**Serves 4-6**

- 2 ounces extra virgin olive oil
- 1 cup onions, very small dice
- ½ cup celery, very small dice
- ½ cup carrots, very small dice
- 3 cloves garlic, very thinly sliced
- ½ pound ground veal
- ½ pound ground pork
- 4 ounces pancetta, ground or finely diced
- 4 ounces (⅔ can) tomato paste
- ½ cup whole milk
- ½ cup dry white wine
- ¼ cup chicken stock or broth
- ½ teaspoon fresh thyme (remove leaves from stem and mince)
- ¼ teaspoon fresh oregano, minced
- Pinch of red pepper flakes (add more if desired)
- Parmesan, shaved
- Salt and pepper as needed
- 1 tablespoon butter

## Instructions

1. Heat large shallow saucepan over medium-low heat. Add olive oil, onions, celery, carrots, and a pinch of salt. Sweat until translucent (approximately 10 minutes) stirring occasionally (do not brown).

2. Add garlic and continue to sweat for 2 minutes.

3. Turn stove to high heat and add veal, pork and pancetta. Brown the meat breaking it up while combining with onions, celery and carrots.

4. Once meat is browned, add tomato paste, wine and milk. Bring to a boil.

5. Add chicken stock, thyme, oregano, and a pinch of red pepper flakes. Bring to boil then reduce heat to medium-low and simmer for 1-1 ½ hours uncovered, stirring occasionally.

6. Season with salt and pepper to taste.

7. Finish with butter.

8. For Neil's Fresh Pasta Recipe visit: www.Loukoumi.com

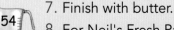

# Vegetable Soup

## Florence Henderson
*Actress*

*"My Dad made vegetable soup and any fresh vegetables that were available went into the soup, along with chicken or maybe a beef bone. We were a poor family, but that soup tasted delicious and always made me feel good, and to this day I love vegetable soup."*

*— Florence Henderson*

## Ingredients

- Any seasonal vegetables
- Onions
- Tomatoes
- Potatoes
- Pinto beans
- Chicken or maybe a beef bone stock
- Salt and pepper

## Instructions

1. Put a pot with water on the stove.

2. Chop up the onions, tomatoes, potatoes and any seasonal vegetables that you like, and add to pot.

3. Add the chicken or beef bone stock, pinto beans, salt and pepper.

4. Simmer until cooked.

# Miranda's Meatloaf

## Miranda Lambert

### Grammy Award Winning Country Music Star

*"I'm all about 'comfort food' and no one does it better than my Mom. One of my favorites is her meatloaf and mashed potatoes. Growing up with private detectives for parents, we never knew who would be at our dinner table — from friends and family to domestic violence victims my parents brought in. One thing for sure, we would have a great meal and good conversation."*

*— Miranda Lambert*

### Ingredients

- 2 pounds ground beef
- 1 pound ground breakfast sausage (mild or regular)
- ½ sleeve of finely crushed saltines or Ritz crackers
- 2 eggs
- 1 dash of Worcestershire Sauce
- 1 teaspoon prepared mustard
- ½ cup brown sugar
- ¼ cup ketchup
- ½ cup finely chopped bell pepper
- ½ finely chopped onion

**Topping:**
- 1 cup ketchup
- ¼ cup brown sugar

### Instructions

1. Mix all the above ingredients together (best option: dig in with both hands!).

2. Put into a baking dish (casserole or loaf style). Bake at 350 degrees for 1 hour.

3. Prepare topping while baking. Topping: Blend together 1 cup ketchup and ¼ cup brown sugar. After baking, pour grease off of loaf. Spread topping over meat generously (If using a large pan you may need extra; use ratio above). Place pan back in the oven for 15 minutes to bake. Let cool for 5-10 minutes before cutting.

ENJOY!

# Beanie Weenie Stew

## Matt Lauer
### Co-Anchor, *The TODAY Show*

*"What kid doesn't like hot dogs? Mix them with baked beans and brown sugar, and it's like dinner and dessert in one! Perfect for a snow day, summer day, any day!"*

*— Matt Lauer*

## Ingredients

- 2 tablespoons vegetable oil
- ½ yellow onion, finely chopped (about 1 cup)
- 3 carrots, peeled and thinly sliced into coins (about 1 cup)
- 1 cup chicken or vegetable broth
- 2 tablespoons yellow mustard
- 2 tablespoons light brown sugar
- ⅓ cup traditional molasses
- 8 ounces hot dogs, sliced into ¼ inch thick coins (about 5 hot dogs)
- Two 16 ounce cans classic baked beans

## Instructions

1. In a large saucepan, heat the oil over medium heat. Add the onions, and cook until softened, stirring occasionally, about 5 minutes.

2. Add the carrots and cook 1 minute. Add the broth, and simmer another 5 minutes.

3. Add the mustard, brown sugar and molasses, and stir to blend well.

4. Add the hot dogs, and simmer 1 minute. Add the baked beans, and simmer another 2-3 minutes.

Yield: 6 to 7 cups of Beanie Weenie Stew, enough for 6 kid-size servings.

# Oyster and Spinach Bisque

## Christian Jules Le Blanc

*Emmy Award Winning Actor,*
*The Young and the Restless*

*"The reason this recipe is one of my favorites is that, not only is it amazingly delicious, but my mother invented it and with it, she won a cooking contest in New Orleans, a town that knows something about great food. She did this while working full time and raising 6 kids. It was one of my first lessons regarding passion and how it transforms, what for some people can be a mundane task, into a great art. My mother was the first artist I ever knew."*

*— Christian Jules Le Blanc*

### Ingredients

- 24 ounces of oysters
- 1 pound frozen chopped spinach
- 4 tablespoons oleo or butter
- ½ cup onion, chopped
- 2 ribs of celery, chopped
- 4 tablespoons flour
- ½ teaspoon garlic salt
- 1 quart evaporated milk
- Pinch of nutmeg
- 1 ½ cups oyster liquid or water
- Salt and pepper to taste
- Liquid from spinach

### Instructions

1. Drain liquid from oysters. Save 1 ½ cups.

2. Cook oysters until well done. Chop oysters.

3. Cook spinach according to label on package. Drain spinach and also save the liquid.

4. Melt oleo or butter over medium heat.

5. Cook onions and celery, stirring. Push onions and celery to side of pan and sprinkle flour over oleo. Stir to make a paste.

6. Pour in oyster and spinach liquid. Stir until smooth. Add oysters and spinach to simmering liquid. Add garlic salt, nutmeg, salt and pepper to taste.

7. Cook uncovered for about 20 minutes. Slowly add a quart of evaporated milk and cook 5 to 10 minutes longer.

# Chicken Enchiladas

## Mario Lopez
*Host, Extra*

*"I really love this Chicken Enchilada recipe. Delicious, healthy style Mexican food is my favorite! Plus, it's quick and easy to make."*
— *Mario Lopez*

## Ingredients
**Serves: 3**
- 6 corn tortillas
- 2 teaspoons olive oil
- ½ cup diced bell pepper
- ½ cup diced onion
- ½ teaspoon salt
- ½ teaspoon dried oregano
- 6 ounces cooked chicken breast, shredded

- 2 tablespoons canned green chilies
- 1 cup mild salsa, divided
- 2 cups baby spinach
- ½ cup low-fat shredded cheese (cheddar or Monterey Jack recommended)
- Chopped scallions
- Hot sauce (optional)
- Nonstick cooking spray

## Instructions

1. Preheat oven to 375 degrees. Wrap tortillas in aluminum foil and place in the oven to warm.

2. Heat oil in a large skillet over medium heat; add onions and peppers. Season with salt and oregano and sauté for 5 minutes. Add chicken, green chilies, ½ cup salsa, and spinach and cook until spinach is wilted.

3. Remove tortillas from the oven and spray a 9x9 inch baking dish with nonstick cooking spray. Place ¼ cup of chicken mixture in tortilla, roll up and transfer to baking dish; repeat with remaining tortillas.

4. Top tortillas with remaining salsa and cheese and bake for 10 minutes until cheese is melted.

5. Garnish with chopped scallions and serve with hot sauce, if desired.

# Chicken Cacciatore

## Evan Lysacek

*2010 Olympic Gold Medalist,*
*Men's Figure Skating*

*"This is a favorite recipe that my mother used to make."*
*— Evan Lysacek*

### Ingredients

- A 3 ½ to 4 pound chicken cut into 8 pieces
- 2 to 3 tablespoons flour for dredging
- ¼ cup extra virgin olive oil
- 3 tablespoons chopped shallots
- 3 minced garlic cloves
- ¼ cup tomato paste
- ½ cup dry white wine
- 1 teaspoon kosher salt
- ¼ teaspoon freshly ground pepper
- ¾ cup chicken stock
- 2 ripe tomatoes, coarsely chopped
- ½ teaspoon red pepper flakes
- ½ bay leaf
- Pinch of thyme
- ½ teaspoon basil
- ½ pound white mushrooms, quartered
- 1 bell pepper cut into large chunks
- 12 jumbo pitted black olives
- 1 onion, sliced thin

### Instructions

1. Dredge chicken with flour and sauté over medium heat in olive oil with shallots and garlic until golden brown.

2. Add the tomato paste, dry white wine, kosher salt, freshly ground pepper, chicken stock, 2 ripe tomatoes coarsely chopped, red pepper flakes, bay leaf, a pinch of thyme, basil, white mushrooms, bell pepper cut into large chunks, 12 jumbo pitted black olives and the sliced onion.

3. Simmer the chicken covered for about an hour or until tender.

4. Serve over thick egg noodles.

 Enjoy :)

# Greek Lemon Roasted Potatoes

## Constantine Maroulis
### American Idol; Tony Nominee, Rock of Ages

*"Ahhh! Mom's potato recipe... Just filled up the house with that great lemony smell. :) Smells like family dinner."*

*— Constantine Maroulis*

### Ingredients
- 3 pounds baking potatoes, peeled and cut into quarter wedges
- ½ cup olive oil
- 1 cup water
- 4 garlic cloves, minced
- 1 ½ teaspoons dried oregano
- 2 bay leaves
- 1 teaspoon coarse salt
- Freshly ground black pepper, to taste
- 1 ½ lemons

### Instructions
1. Preheat the oven to 400 degrees. Place potatoes in a single layer in a roasting pan and toss with the olive oil, water, garlic, oregano and bay leaves.

2. Season with salt and pepper and give everything a toss until well coated. Squeeze one lemon over the potatoes. Then place the squeezed halves on top.

3. Bake the potatoes until they appear to be golden brown and tender, about 40 minutes. Shake the pan from time to time to ensure even cooking, but be careful not to break the tender potatoes. If pan appears dry add additional ½ cup water. Bake for an additional 40 minutes or until fork tender. Potatoes can be broiled at the final end of cooking for 2 to 3 minutes or until golden brown and crisp on edges.

4. To serve, remove the bay leaves and lemon halves. Squeeze with additional ½ lemon. Taste for seasoning, adding additional salt and pepper, if necessary. Serve at once.

# Sweet Potato Poon

## Al Roker

*Co-Anchor, The TODAY Show*

*"This is something my Mom used to make every Thanksgiving and Christmas. Even though she's gone now, every time I make it, it reminds me of my mother."*

*– Al Roker*

### Ingredients

- 6 large sweet potatoes
- 4 teaspoons baking powder
- 1 teaspoon salt
- 1 stick of unsalted butter
- 1 cup of flour
- 1 cup of dark brown sugar
- 1 can of crushed pineapple, drained
- 1 teaspoon cinnamon
- 1 teaspoon nutmeg
- 1 teaspoon allspice
- 1 bag of large Jet Puffed marshmallows

### Instructions

1. Boil the sweet potatoes until soft.

2. Mash potatoes with 1 stick of butter in a large bowl.

3. Add flour, sugar, salt, baking powder, cinnamon, nutmeg, allspice and mix together. Fold in crushed pineapple and pour into a buttered 9" x 12" Pyrex dish.

4. Bake in a 350 degree oven for 30 minutes or until brown on top.

5. Remove from oven, layer with marshmallows and place under broiler until marshmallows are toasty brown on top.

BE CAREFUL! THEY WILL CATCH FIRE VERY QUICKLY...A TRADITION IN THE ROKER HOUSEHOLD FOR GENERATIONS!

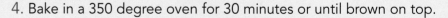

# Sunday Sauce with Meatballs, Sausages & Pork Chops

## The Scotto Family

*FRESCO by Scotto Restaurant;*
*FRESCO on the go*

*"Sunday has always been a very special day in our home. My earliest memories involve making meatballs with my Grandfather early Sunday morning. The tradition continues with my father, my kids and all his grandchildren making the Sunday sauce. Calories are not counted!"*

— *Rosanna Scotto, Good Day New York Anchor*

## Ingredients

**Serving Size**: 8 very hungry people
**Meatballs**
- 2 pounds ground beef
- 2 slices American bread
- ½ cup of milk
- 1 cup finely chopped onion
- 3 tablespoons chopped fresh parsley
- 2 eggs
- 4 tablespoons grated Parmesan cheese

- 1 ½ tablespoons chopped garlic
- 3 tablespoons olive oil
- Salt and pepper to taste
- 2 cups tomato sauce, warmed

**Pork Chops**
- ½ cup extra-virgin olive oil
- 1 pound sausage, mild
- ½ pound hot Italian sausage
- 6 thinly sliced pork chops (about 3 pounds)
- 2 cups dry red wine

- 2 tablespoons chopped garlic
- 2 onions, diced
- 1 cup pancetta, diced
- 1 tablespoon crushed red pepper
- 1 gallon Italian tomatoes
- Salt to taste
- 2 cups chopped basil
- 2 pounds cooked meatballs
- 1 pound uncooked rigatoni

## Instructions

1. **For the Meatballs:** Soak the bread in the milk. In a medium bowl, mix the ground beef, bread, onions, parsley, eggs, cheese and garlic. Add salt and pepper to taste. If the mixture is dry, add ½ cup of cold water and mix well. Form into about 12 meatballs. Place the meatballs in a sauté pan with the olive oil and fry over medium heat until brown, 10 to 15 minutes.

2. **For the Pork Chops:** In a large pot over medium heat, heat the oil and sauté the sausage and pork chops until brown, about 10 minutes. Don't worry if the meat is not cooked through because it will cook through in the sauce. Remove the meat from the pan and set aside. Deglaze the pan with 1 cup red wine.

3. In the same pot, add the garlic, onions, pancetta, and crushed red pepper and cook until the onions and garlic are lightly browned, about 2 minutes. Add the remaining cup of red wine and reduce by half. Add the tomatoes and salt and simmer for 1 hour over low heat. Add the basil, sausage, pork chops, and meatballs to the tomato sauce and simmer for an additional hour over low heat.

4. In a large pot of boiling, salted water, cook the pasta for 10 to 12 minutes or until *al dente*. Drain the pasta, toss it with the Sunday Sauce and serve immediately.

# Chicken Pesto Pasta

## Sherri Shepherd

*Co-Host, The View;*
*Host, The Newlywed Game*

*"This was my favorite childhood recipe because it was the first recipe I learned how to make, and it was easy for me and my sisters to make dinner when our parents weren't home."*

— *Sherri Shepherd*

### Ingredients

- 1 pound cooked chicken breast
- 1 box of spaghetti
- 2 cups packed fresh basil leaves
- 1/3 cup pine nuts
- 1/3 cup extra virgin olive oil
- 3 medium garlic cloves
- Salt and freshly ground black pepper, to taste

### Instructions

1. Cook pasta according to package directions.

2. Combine ingredients in food processor (except the pasta and the chicken breast) to make the pesto. Pulse to combine. Process until desired consistency.

3. Drain spaghetti; transfer to large bowl. Add pesto; toss to coat.

4. Add cubed or shredded cooked chicken breast.

SPAGHETTI

# Greens & Beans

## Dylan & Cole Sprouse

*Actors, The Suite Life on Deck*

*"As children, our Dad cooked for us a lot, and though we loved all his meals, there was one in particular we always looked forward to. Our Dad calls it Greens and Beans, and it's a Sprouse family recipe."*
*— Dylan & Cole Sprouse*

### Ingredients
- 2 large heads of escarole
- 2 cans of Great Northern white beans
- 1 package of fresh Italian sausage
- 2 quarts of chicken broth

### Instructions

1. To prepare you must cut up and brown your sausage (drain sausage grease if wanted after).

2. Once drained, add Great Northern white beans and let simmer for 2 minutes (do not drain beans).

3. Add the chicken broth, then proceed to chop the escarole. Once chopped, use a strainer to wash the escarole of impurities, then proceed to add the escarole to the pot.

4. Add the lid to the pot (preferably a large stew pot) and let simmer on low heat for half an hour. Once done, serve!

"And there you have it, the patented Sprouse family Greens and Beans recipe. Enjoy!"

# Sunday Sauce

## George Stephanopoulos
### Anchor, Good Morning America

*"On Sunday afternoons I like to relax in the kitchen, but there are few things I cook that my kids will eat. Here's the exception: a Bolognese with a Greek twist (the cinnamon!) that my daughters Elliott, 9, and Harper, 6, call 'Daddy's Sauce.'"*

*— George Stephanopoulos*

## Ingredients
**Serves: 6**

- 3 medium sweet onions
- 3 carrots
- 3 celery stalks
- 1 tablespoon garlic, chopped
- 4 strips thick bacon
- 1 ½ pounds ground pork
- ½ pound ground veal
- 1 large can plum tomatoes
- 1 cinnamon stick
- 3 ounces milk
- 3 tablespoons olive oil
- Salt and pepper

## Instructions

1. Chop vegetables and bacon.

2. Brown bacon until crisp. Add oil and brown garlic. Then add onions. Sauté slowly over medium heat (10-15 minutes). Add carrots and celery. Sauté another 5-10 minutes.

3. Brown meat in a separate pan, seasoned with salt and pepper. Then fold in vegetables for another 5-10 minutes. Crush tomatoes by hand over meat and vegetables. When whole mixture is bubbling add milk and cinnamon stick.

4. Stir, cover, reduce heat to simmer and cook for an additional 1-3 hours.

5. Serve with any kind of pasta. It definitely improves if you refrigerate overnight.

# Corn Pudding

## Marlo Thomas

*Actress & National Outreach Director,
St. Jude Children's Research Hospital®*

*"All of the kids in our family love this delicious corn pudding that my Mom used to make for us. It is rich in flavor and warms your heart. It is always a favorite at our family gatherings."*

*— Marlo Thomas*

### Ingredients
- 1 can whole kernel corn
- 2 cans creamed corn
- 2 boxes of corn muffin mix
- 2 sticks salted butter, melted
- 1 pint sour cream

### Instructions
1. Mix all ingredients.
2. Cook at 350 degrees for 45 minutes or until firm.

67

# Delicious Desserts

# Ernie's Super Grape Nut Pudding

## Ernie Anastos
*FOX News Anchor*

*"Family is the center of life, and the center of home is the kitchen! As a child and later as a parent, my fondest memories revolve around special food dishes. These tasty experiences are certainly prepared with a lot of care and love. So, let me share one of my favorites that I hope will bring good news to you and your family."*

*— Ernie Anastos*

### Ingredients
- 3 cups milk
- ½ cup Grape Nuts cereal
- 3 eggs
- ½ cup sugar
- ½ teaspoon cinnamon
- 1 teaspoon vanilla extract

### Instructions

1. Beat eggs and sugar, then add the rest of the ingredients.

2. Mix well. Pour into a 1 quart soufflé dish.

3. Place in a larger pan and pour hot water around dish.

4. Bake in a pre-heated 350 degree oven for 1 hour.

5. Enjoy my super treat!

# Brownies & Lemon Squares

## Katie Couric

*TV Personality; ABC News Contributor*

> *"These simple recipes are my go-to when I need something to satisfy my sweet tooth. My daughters love them too!"*
>
> *— Katie Couric*

### Ingredients

**Brownies:**

- 2 squares unsweetened chocolate
- ¼ pound butter or margarine, melted in a saucepan
- Dash of salt
- 1 cup sugar
- 2 eggs
- ½ cup flour
- 1 cup nuts
- 1 teaspoon vanilla

### Instructions

1. Preheat oven to 350 degrees.
2. Melt chocolate and butter in a saucepan.
3. Add a dash of salt.
4. Beat 1 cup of sugar, 2 eggs for 2 minutes.
5. Add ½ cup of flour, 1 cup of nuts, 1 teaspoon vanilla.
6. Bake in oven at 350 degrees for 25-30 minutes (toothpick check). Cool and cut. Makes about 16 brownies.

### Ingredients

**Lemon Squares:**

Crust:

- 1 cup butter
- ½ cup confectioners' sugar
- 2 cups flour
- Pinch of salt

Filling:

- 4 eggs
- 2 cups sugar
- 6 tablespoons flour
- 6 tablespoons lemon juice
- Grated rind of one lemon

### Instructions

1. Preheat oven to 350 degrees.
2. (CRUST): Blend dry ingredients, cut in butter until mixture is crumbly.
3. Press into oblong, lightly greased baking pan.
4. Bake 20 minutes at 350 degrees.
5. (FILLING): Mix with beater: eggs, sugar, flour, lemon juice - add grated rind, spread on top of baked crust. Bake for 25 minutes at 350 degrees.
6. When cool, sprinkle with confectioners' sugar. Cut into squares.

**REMEMBER:** Pan should be larger than a cake pan - bars are better a little thinner, than thick.

70

# Brown Sugar Cookies

## Marcia Cross

*Actress, Desperate Housewives*

*"My mother's yummy brown sugar cookies...with milk. Heaven."*
*— Marcia Cross*

### Ingredients
- 1 pound brown sugar
- ½ pound margarine (2 sticks)
- 2 eggs
- 3 ½ cups flour
- 1 teaspoon baking soda
- 1 cup chopped nuts, optional

### Instructions

1. Beat sugar, margarine and eggs until creamy. Add flour and baking soda and mix well.

2. Pack into loaf pan and chill several hours or overnight.

3. Slice and bake at 350 degrees, approximately 6 minutes, or as needed.

4. Sprinkle with nuts if desired.

# Peanut Butter Balls

## Paula Deen
*Celebrity Chef/Author*

*"When I make Peanut Butter Balls it takes me back to my childhood, when I was just a little girl who loved this dish so much and wanted nothing more in the world than to eat it every day!"*

— *Paula Deen*

### Ingredients
**Makes 18 to 24 pieces**
- 1 cup peanut butter
- 1 cup honey
- 2 cups powdered milk

- 1 ½ cups crushed corn flakes, or
- 1 ½ cups finely chopped walnuts or pecans, or
- 1 cup powdered sugar

### Instructions
1. Mix peanut butter, honey, and milk together in a large bowl to form a very thick mixture.

2. Roll mixture into small balls about the size of a walnut.

3. Roll the balls in either the crushed corn flakes, finely chopped nuts, or powdered sugar.

4. Place on waxed paper and refrigerate for 20 minutes.

# Christmas Spritz Cookies

## Frank Dicopoulos

*Actor, Guiding Light*

> *"These 'Christmas Spritz Cookies' are from my wife Teja's mother, Peggy Anderson and grandmother Hilma Bennett. Teja and I have passed this recipe on to our own family for the past 20 years. This recipe is over 75 years old!"*
>
> *— Frank Dicopoulos*

### Ingredients
- 2 ½ cups flour
- ½ teaspoon baking powder
- 1 cup butter (or margarine)
- ¾ cup sugar
- 1 teaspoon vanilla
- Dash of salt
- 1 egg unbeaten (or egg substitute)

### Instructions
1. Sift flour with baking powder.

2. Cream butter, sugar and salt.

3. Add egg and vanilla. Beat well!

4. Add sifted ingredients in small amounts.

5. Mold with cookie press on cold, ungreased pans.

6. Bake in 375 degree oven for 12 to 15 minutes.

7. Flavor can be changed by adding grated orange or lemon rind.

# No-Bake Peanut Butter Oatmeal Cookies

## Mike Emanuel

### *Chief Congressional Correspondent, Fox News*

*"I love this recipe because kids of all ages love yummy cookies! Plus, other than getting some help from Mom or Dad with boiling the ingredients, a child can be very involved with this cookie creation."*

— Mike Emanuel

### Ingredients
- 2 cups sugar
- ¼ cup cocoa
- ½ cup milk
- ½ cup butter
- 1 teaspoon vanilla
- ½ cup peanut butter (chunky or smooth)
- 3 cups quick cook oats

### Instructions
1. In a heavy saucepan, mix together sugar, cocoa, milk and butter.
2. Cook over medium heat until mixture starts to boil.
3. Remove pan from heat and cool for 1 minute.
4. Add vanilla, peanut butter and oatmeal.
5. Stir completely until peanut butter is melted and oatmeal is coated.
6. Drop by teaspoonful onto wax paper.
7. Cool completely.
8. Store in an airtight container.

Photo: John Russo

# My Nonna's Italian Cookies

## David Henrie

*Actor, Wizards of Waverly Place*

*"Christmas is not Christmas without my Nonna's cookies."*
— *David Henrie*

### Ingredients
- 5 cups all-purpose flour
- 1 cup sugar
  (blend)
- 2 tablespoons vanilla extract
- 2 sticks butter, melted
- 2 tablespoons baking powder
- 1 cup whole milk
- 5 eggs

### Instructions
1. Mix ingredients until doughy. Roll into different shapes or as individual balls.

2. Place in 375 degree oven for 20 minutes (or until cookies have started to turn a golden brown).

3. Once cookies are made and cooled, add icing on top.

### Icing Ingredients
- 1 tablespoon butter
- ¼ cup milk
- 1 cup powdered sugar

### Instructions
Make icing in a small pan on the stove. Blend until you have a slightly thick consistency. You may need to add more or less milk and powdered sugar. Sprinkles on top (optional).

# Faith's Coca-Cola Cake

## Faith Hill

*Grammy Award Winning Entertainer*

*"I love this Coca-Cola Cake. It is so rich and decadent...you need to drink a lot of milk with it!"*

*— Faith Hill*

### Ingredients

**For Cake:**
- 2 cups unsifted flour
- 2 cups sugar
- 2 sticks butter
- 2 tablespoons cocoa
- 1 cup Coca-Cola
- ½ cup buttermilk
- 1 teaspoon baking soda
- 2 eggs, beaten
- 1 tablespoon vanilla
- 1 ½ cups miniature marshmallows

**For Icing:**
- ½ cup butter
- 3 tablespoons cocoa
- 6 tablespoons Coca-Cola
- 16 ounces confectioners' sugar

### Instructions

**For Cake:**

1. Sift flour and sugar in bowl.

2. Heat butter, cocoa and Coca-Cola to boiling point. Pour over flour/sugar mixture.

3. Add buttermilk, baking soda, eggs, vanilla and marshmallows (Batter will be thin and marshmallows will float to top).

4. Pour batter into greased and floured 9x13 inch pan. Bake at 350 degrees for 30-35 minutes.

**Icing:**

1. Combine all ingredients and heat until it boils.

2. Pour over cake while hot.

Photo: Jillian Nelson

# Any Day Sundaes

## The Katsoris Family

Photo: Jillian Nelson

*"There's nothing like sharing a Sundae any day of the week!"*
*—Dean and Nick Katsoris*

## Dean's Ice Cream Sundae

### Ingredients
- Ice cream
- Hershey's chocolate syrup
- Sprinkles
- Maraschino cherries
- Oreo cookies
- Peanuts

### Instructions
1. Scoop 3 scoops of ice cream into a bowl.
2. Squeeze some Hershey's chocolate syrup on top.
3. Add sprinkles.
4. Add peanuts.
5. Crush up 2 Oreo cookies.
6. Add one cherry on top.
7. Make another one for my sister Julia.

## Nick's JELL-O Sundae

### Ingredients
- Sugar free strawberry JELL-O
- Miniature chocolate chips
- Cool Whip
- Graham crackers
- Peanuts

### Instructions
1. Scoop 2 scoops of strawberry JELL-O or use 2 individual sized cups.
2. Put 2 large spoonfuls of Cool Whip on top.
3. Crush up one large graham cracker and add on top of the Cool Whip.
4. Sprinkle a handful of chocolate chips and some peanuts (or even your favorite breakfast cereal) on top.
5. Share with your family!

# Spice Paximathia

## Melina Kanakaredes
*Actress*

*"This is one of my favorite cookie recipes. I used to make them with my Mom and my Yia-Yia (grandmother) and now my girls are making them with me and their Yia-Yia."*

— *Melina Kanakaredes*

## Ingredients

**Makes about 10 dozen**
- ½ cup Mazola Oil
- ½ pound butter (preferably unsalted)
- 2 cups sugar
- 6 eggs, well beaten
- 1 teaspoon vanilla

- 7 cups flour, sifted (approximately)
- 3 teaspoons baking powder
- ½ teaspoon baking soda
- 6-7 teaspoons cinnamon
- 1 teaspoon allspice
- ½ teaspoon cloves

## Instructions

1. Set oven temperature to 375 degrees. Cream oil, butter, and sugar together for 15 minutes.

2. Gradually add eggs to creamed sugar mixture and blend thoroughly. Add vanilla. Sift flour, baking powder, baking soda, and spices together. Slowly add dry ingredients to sugar and egg mixture to make a medium dough that leaves the sides of the bowl.

3. Knead dough slightly. Divide into 5 parts. Shape into long, narrow, flat loaves, about 2 ½" wide and 1" thick.

4. Place on greased cookie sheets 2" apart to allow for baking. Score each loaf in ½" slices. Bake until lightly browned (about 20 minutes).

5. Remove from oven. While still warm, slice where previously scored.

6. Toast slices on both sides in moderate oven until lightly browned. Allow to cool before serving.

# Rice Pudding & Chocolate Crackles

## Nicole Kidman
### *Academy Award Winning Actress*

*"Chocolate Crackles were the ultimate birthday party treat as a child – I loved them! Rice Pudding reminds me so much of my childhood. It was one of my mother's favorites, and now it's one of mine."*

*– Nicole Kidman*

## Ingredients
### RICE PUDDING

- ¼ cup rice
- 2 cups water
- Pinch of salt
- 3 eggs
- ⅓ cup sugar
- 1 tablespoon vanilla essence
- 2 ½ cups milk
- ¼ cup sultanas

## Instructions

1. Preheat the oven to 350 degrees (180 degrees C). Bring the water and salt to a boil, then gradually add the rice. Boil rapidly uncovered for 10 minutes and drain well.

2. Beat eggs, sugar and vanilla together. Add the rice and sultanas. Slowly add the milk and gradually stir to combine evenly.

3. Pour into a shallow ovenproof dish and stand the dish in a baking tin. Fill the baking tin with water so it reaches halfway up the baking dish. Bake in a moderate oven for 30-35 minutes.

4. Stir the rice with a fork to prevent a skin from forming. Reduce heat to 320 degrees (160 degrees C) and bake for a further 30-40 minutes, or until custard is set.

### CHOCOLATE CRACKLES

- About 1 cup (200g) dark chocolate, chopped
- About 1 stick butter (100g)
- ⅓ cup (115g) golden syrup
- 4 cups (140g) puffed rice cereal

1. Place the chocolate, butter and golden syrup in a saucepan over low heat and cook, stirring, until melted and smooth.

2. Place the cereal in a bowl with the chocolate mixture and mix well to combine.

3. Spoon 2 teaspoons of the mixture into 48 small paper cases. Refrigerate for 1 hour or until set. Makes 48.

79

Photo: Yolanda Perez

# Coconut Cake

## Susan Lucci

*Emmy Award Winning Actress, All My Children;*
*Author, All My Life*

*"This cake brings back so many happy memories of my childhood. My grandmother (I called her 'Nana') would make this cake on special occasions. She would make this delicious cake most often at Easter. For my first communion, Nana poured the batter into a lamb mold which made the cake appear in the shape of a lamb and used jelly beans for its eyes. I recall watching her make this cake and the joy she had in doing so. I hope you enjoy it as much as I do!"*

*— Susan Lucci*

### Cake Ingredients
- 2 ¼ cups all-purpose flour
- 1 ½ cups granulated sugar
- 2 ½ teaspoons double-acting baking powder
- 1 teaspoon salt
- Milk
- 3 eggs
- 1 teaspoon orange extract
- ½ teaspoon almond extract
- Two 9" round layer pans (1 ½" deep)
- 1 stick softened butter

### Instructions
1. Preheat oven to 375 degrees.
   Sift: All-purpose flour, sugar, baking powder, salt into mixing bowl.

2. Add: Butter, ½ cup milk, orange extract, almond extract, 1 beaten egg.

3. Beat together 200 strokes by hand or 2 minutes by mixer at low speed.

4. Add: ¼ cup milk, 2 beaten eggs. Beat together 200 strokes by hand or 2 minutes by mixer at low speed.

5. Pour into two round 9" greased layer pans. Bake until cake tests done. Cool and remove from pans. Baking time: 25-30 minutes.

### Best 7 Minute Frosting Ingredients
- 2 unbeaten egg whites
- 1 ½ cups sugar
- 5 tablespoons cold water
- 1 teaspoon light corn syrup
- ⅛ teaspoon salt
- 16 ounces shredded coconut
- ½ teaspoon orange extract
- ½ teaspoon almond extract
- 2 regular size marshmallows, cut in pieces

1. Mix thoroughly on top of double boiler: egg whites, sugar, cold water, light corn syrup, salt. Set over rapidly boiling water and beat constantly with rotary egg beater until mixture will hold a peak for 7 minutes.

2. Add: Orange extract, almond extract, marshmallows. Beat until cool and thick enough to spread frosting between layers and sprinkle ¼ cup of coconut. Spread remaining frosting on top and sides of cake. Pat 1 cup coconut onto sides of cake.

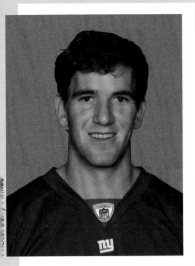

# Lace Cookies

## Eli Manning

*Super Bowl MVP, NY Giants*

*"My mom made these cookies for us all the time and they are my favorite. She still makes them every time I make a visit home."*

*— Eli Manning*

## Ingredients

**Makes about 6 dozen cookies**
- 2 cups Old Fashioned Rolled Oats
- 1 tablespoon flour
- 2 cups white sugar

- ½ teaspoon salt
- 2 sticks melted butter
- 2 eggs, beaten
- 1 teaspoon vanilla

## Instructions

1. Put the oats, flour, sugar and salt into a large bowl and mix well.

2. Pour very hot melted butter over mixture and stir until the sugar has melted.

3. Add eggs and vanilla - stir well.

4. Preheat oven to 325 degrees. Cover cookie sheets with ungreased aluminum foil.

5. Drop ½ level teaspoons of the mixture on foil - 2 inches apart.

6. Cook about 10-12 minutes.

7. Watch carefully – When cookies are completely cooled, foil will peel off.

8. Store in airtight containers.

# Banana Pudding

## Doc Shaw

*Actor, Pair of Kings*

*"It's good during a hot summer's day when you need a sweet treat. Also good at a family gathering. Just make sure they don't take it all!"*
— *Doc Shaw*

### Ingredients
- JELL-O Banana Pudding Mix
- Bananas
- Vanilla Wafers
- Milk
- Cool Whip

### Instructions

1. Follow directions on the package of the banana pudding mix.

2. Add bananas, Cool Whip and Vanilla Wafers.

3. Mix that bad boy up and you've got a dessert that is scrumdiddlyumpcious!

# Marshmallow Fruit Salad

## Tiffany Thornton
*Actress, So Random!*

*"When I was growing up I loved sweets so my mom and grandmother made up this recipe as a way of incorporating sweets and fruits. My grandfather and I LOVE this dessert. Pops actually loves it so much he wakes up in the middle of the night and eats the oranges out of it. The evidence is always there the next day - haha."*

*— Tiffany Thornton*

## Ingredients
- 1 small bag mini marshmallows
- 1 large can crushed pineapple, drained
- 1 cup coconut (optional)
- 1 cup chopped pecans (optional)
- 1 cup sour cream
- 1 large can Mandarin oranges, drained

## Instructions
1. Combine sour cream, crushed pineapple, marshmallows and coconut, if you'd like. Mix together in large mixing bowl. Add pecans. Mix. Last add Mandarin oranges.

2. Flavor is best when it sits overnight in the fridge, but if you are like me you can just stick it in the fridge while you eat dinner, and then have it for dessert :)

(If you'd like it sweeter, you can add a smidgen of vanilla to the sour cream).

Enjoy!

# Granny's Coconut Cake

## Justin Timberlake
### Grammy and Emmy Award Winning Singer/Actor

*"My favorite part of going home has always been my Granny's cooking. She is an amazing cook. This is the most wonderful coconut cake ever! It's even good for breakfast the next morning (Followed by a nice week long diet!!!)."*

*— Justin Timberlake*

## Ingredients
- 1 box white cake mix
- 2 cups of granulated sugar
- 8 ounces of sour cream
- 3 packages of frozen flake coconut (if you can't find frozen flake coconut, substitute Baker's Angel Flake Sweetened Coconut)

## Instructions
1. Start with a box of white cake mix. Prepare cake mix according to package directions, using two 8 or 9-inch round pans. Once cakes are cool, slice in half to form four layers.

2. For the icing, mix together sugar, sour cream and 2 packages of frozen flake coconut.

3. Spread between layers and over top and sides of cake.

4. Use the remaining package of coconut to cover the top and sides of the cake.

# Cowboy Cookies

## Reese Witherspoon
### *Academy Award Winning Actress*

*"I never met a cookie I didn't like. These are my absolute favorite!"*
*— Reese Witherspoon*

## Ingredients

- 1 cup margarine
- 1 cup brown sugar
- 1 cup sugar
- 1 teaspoon vanilla
- 2 cups flour
- ½ teaspoon baking powder
- 1 teaspoon baking soda
- 1 teaspoon salt
- 1 teaspoon cinnamon
- 1 cup chopped nuts
- 2 cups oatmeal
- ½ cup coconut
- 2 eggs

## Instructions

1. Cream together margarine, sugars, eggs and vanilla.

2. Sift flour, baking powder, baking soda, salt and cinnamon together. Add to first mixture and mix thoroughly.

3. Fold in remaining ingredients.

4. Drop on greased cookie sheets.

5. Bake at 350 degrees until golden brown.

*Put your photo here*

# My Favorite Childhood Recipe

**(Insert Your Name)**
*Junior Chef*

Ingredients

Instructions

# Allergy-Friendly Ingredient Substitutes
# From 2 Moms Who Know (and Care!)
## Suggested by: Voula Katsoris and
## Lori Sandler, Founder of Divvies

Photo: Bob Rozycki

There are many delicious products available free of the 8 most common allergens (peanuts, tree nuts, dairy, eggs, fish, wheat, shellfish, and soy) that may be substituted for ingredients deemed off limits to those with food allergies/intolerances. If you are uncertain that a particular substitution will work in a recipe, we suggest you cut the recipe in half as you experiment. Always be certain to read and re-read labels every time you shop and/or cook as manufacturers occasionally change ingredients and production practices. These suggested brands were free of certain allergens at time of printing. Enjoy!

**Butter:** Earth Balance Vegan Buttery Sticks, Fleischmann's Unsalted Margarine, Earth Balance Natural Shortening, Earth Balance Soy Free Natural Buttery Spread.

**Buttermilk:** Make your own by placing 1 tablespoon plain white vinegar into 1 cup of soy or rice milk. Let the mixture stand for 5 to 10 minutes before using.

**Cheese:** Tofutti cheeses. Tofutti American flavored slices are great for grilled cheese sandwiches! Galaxy Nutritional Foods (Vegan and Rice Vegan) brand cheeses are also delicious options.

**Chocolate:** Divvies Divvine Chocolate Bars, Benjamint Crunch Bars, and Semi-Sweet Chocolate Chips, and Enjoy Life Foods' Chocolate Chunks and Chips for baking.

**Egg:** Ener-G Egg Replacer; or ¼ cup unsweetened apple sauce per egg; or 1 teaspoon white vinegar per egg; or 1 tablespoon pureed silken tofu per egg (be sure to strain excess liquid).

**Gluten-Free Flour Blend:** There are plenty of gluten-free flour blends available in grocery stores.

**Heavy cream:** Make your own by pureeing silken tofu in a blender and thinning with soy or rice milk until desired consistency is achieved.

**Ice Cream:** SO Delicious dairy-free frozen desserts, Rice Dream non-dairy frozen dessert and Tofutti non-dairy frozen dessert.

**Milk:** Rice milk and soy milk.

**Peanut butter:** Soy nut butter and sunflower seed butter.

**Sour cream and Cream Cheese:** Tofutti's Better than Sour Cream & Better than Cream Cheese (made from tofu). You can also try Galaxy Nutritional Foods Vegan brand cream cheese.

**Yogurt:** Soy and/or coconut milk yogurts. Silk and SO Delicious are great choices!

**For more information about food allergies and allergy-friendly recipes, visit FAAN at www.foodallergy.org**

## About the Author

*Loukoumi's Celebrity Cookbook* is Nick Katsoris' fifth book in the Loukoumi series. Other titles include the iParenting Media Award winning: *Loukoumi, Growing up with Loukoumi, Loukoumi's Good Deeds* and *Loukoumi's Gift*. The books have been translated into Greek by Livanis Publishing in Athens. Katsoris sponsors the annual *Growing Up With Loukoumi Dream Day* contest which grants kids the opportunity to spend the day in their dream careers. He also sponsors *Make A Difference With Loukoumi Day*, based on his book *Loukoumi's Good Deeds,* which rallies thousands of kids each October to do a good deed on *National Make A Difference Day*. Katsoris is a New York attorney as General Counsel of the Red Apple Group, and President of the Hellenic Times Scholarship Fund, which has awarded over 700 scholarships. Nick is also author of the legal thriller *Crimes of Fire*. He currently resides in Eastchester, New York, with his wife, Voula, a real estate attorney, and their children, Dean and Julia.

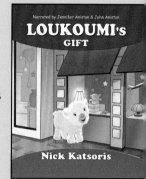

*Loukoumi's Good Deeds* and *Loukoumi's Gift* are
narrated on CD by Jennifer Aniston & John Aniston
Alexis Christoforous, Frank Dicopoulos, Olympia Dukakis,
Gloria Gaynor, Constantine Maroulis & featuring
Gloria Gaynor's original song "Make Someone Smile"

*$2 from the sale of each book will be donated to St. Jude Children's Research Hospital®*

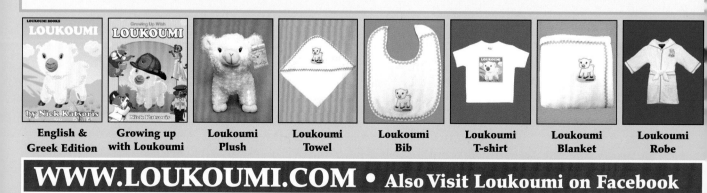

| English & Greek Edition | Growing up with Loukoumi | Loukoumi Plush | Loukoumi Towel | Loukoumi Bib | Loukoumi T-shirt | Loukoumi Blanket | Loukoumi Robe |